THE WACKY DISCOVERIES OF GEORGE WA

By Karen Clopton-Dunson

A **special thanks** to George Washington Carver for giving me a fun story to tell, Lenora Collier for sowing the first seed into my vision and my mother, Harriett Carter who taught me to love and appreciate my heritage.

Something had gone terribly wrong
In my small, friendly home town.
I was awakened by farmers.
Each face was wearing a frown.

Mr. George Washington Carver!!!"
I heard a farmer yell.
"You told us to plant peanuts,
But the peanuts won't even sell."

I was frozen in my tracks,
When I heard tiny chatter.

"Hey don't you dare step on me!
I heard a peanut say.
"I'm worth a lot around here."
I politely stepped out of the way.

"Take a good look at me.
I'm more than a nut to eat.
If you take me to your lab,
My secrets will be your treat."

It was a terrific idea!
A solution had to be found.
So I pulled...................

And pulled

And pulled

Until........

....The plant **popped** out of the ground.

I scooped peanuts in my pocket.
They were quite a lively bunch.

When I packed them in my hat,
I heard some of them go **Crunch.**

I hurried to my science lab
And secretly locked the door.*
I did not fully realize
What my life was headed for.

One climbed in my grinding machine.
Another turned on the power.

When I tried to rescue him,
He had turned into flour.

Peanuts were being chased
By Tusky, my hungry cat.
They bravely jumped off the counter.
I heard each of them go splat.

I spread the splatter on fresh bread.
Words were so hard to utter.
I smiled to myself and declared,
" I'll call it peanut butter."

Peanuts divided into chemicals.
There was very little hope.
When they finally climbed out,
They had transformed into soap.

Peanuts playfully squirted oil.
The oil landed in my cup.

I added some salt and sugar.
Mmmmm, milk! We drank it all up.

This big mess the peanuts made
Did not look very funny.
I tripped and fell, trying hard
To capture oil that was runny.

I added two wild, sweet berries.
What a discovery I made!

Wowie! I re-created
The world's greatest lemonade.

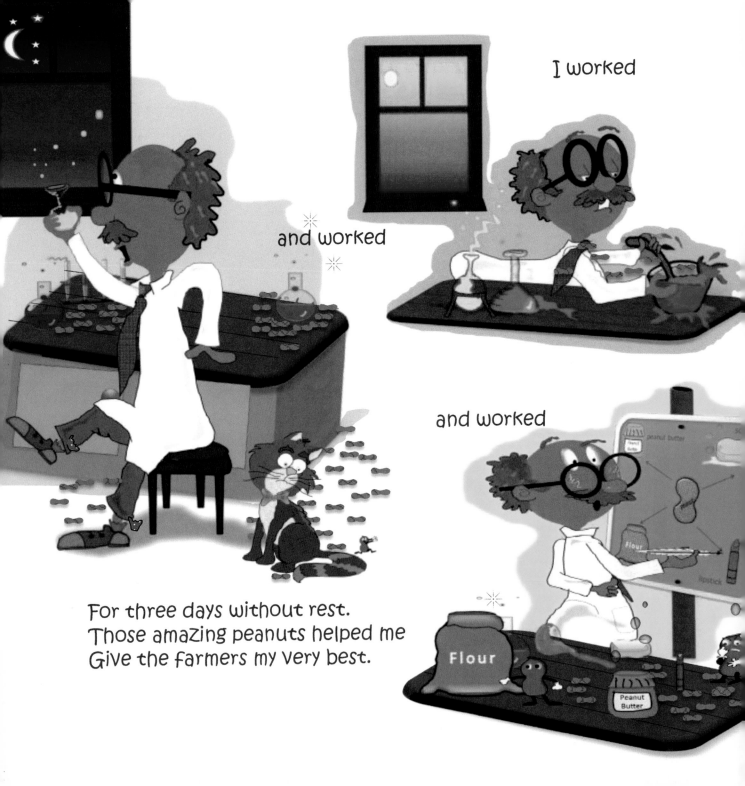

I worked

and worked

and worked

For three days without rest.
Those amazing peanuts helped me
Give the farmers my very best.

I turned off the light.

And dashed out the door.
I had loads of good stuff.
Who would dare ask for more?

I had coffee, peanut butter,
Soap, cheese and a soft drink,
Lipstick, face powder
Hair shampoo and even some ink.

Ice-cream, flour, butter and milk
And some polish for your shoe.
These are just a few samples
From peanuts the farmers grew.

I'll never forget what happened
On those three magical days.
Together we saved the farmers
In the most peculiar ways.

The End

Karen Clopton-Dunson

has taught kindergarten and Head start in the Chicago Public School system. Teaching the history of Africans in America inspired her to write history books with clever rhymes and quirky illustrations to captivate, inspire and educate beginning readers. The author lives in Chicago. This is her first children's book.

Another Fun History Book:
Doctor Daniel Hale Williams in Twas the Night of a Miracle

Made in the USA
Coppell, TX
27 November 2019